YOUR KNOWLEDGE HAS VALUE

Bibliographic information published by the German National Library:

The German National Library lists this publication in the National Bibliography; detailed bibliographic data are available on the Internet at http://dnb.dnb.de .

Imprint:

Copyright © 2017 GRIN Verlag, Open Publishing GmbH
Print and binding: Books on Demand GmbH, Norderstedt Germany
ISBN: 9783668558465

This book at GRIN:

http://www.grin.com/en/e-book/377643/admisabilty-of-dna-and-digital-evidence-in-zimbabwe

Talent Chipandu

Admisabilty of DNA and digital evidence in Zimbabwe

GRIN Publishing

GRIN - Your knowledge has value

Since its foundation in 1998, GRIN has specialized in publishing academic texts by students, college teachers and other academics as e-book and printed book. The website www.grin.com is an ideal platform for presenting term papers, final papers, scientific essays, dissertations and specialist books.

Visit us on the internet:

http://www.grin.com/

http://www.facebook.com/grincom

http://www.twitter.com/grin_com

The law of evidence in Zimbabwe is concerned with how information is presented and circumstances under which it can be excluded in a court of law. It is concerned with the relevance and admissibility of evidence in court. The law of evidence is used in both criminal and civil matters. It is common to human nature that when times change, there are new crimes that are committed and new areas of dispute which arise. The law must move with the changing times and address the new legal issues that come up. The introduction and adoption of digital and DNA evidence is an answer to modern day challenges and the need to ensure that justice is served. In Zimbabwe, the laws which provide for the admission of digital and DNA evidence are skeletal in nature except in criminal matter in relation to DNA. Due to other factors like poor technological advancements it is left to the court to determine the admissibility and relevance of evidence in the form of digital and DNA evidence. The legislature and courts are gradually moving towards an era where digital and DNA evidence become independent forms of evidence. In as much as progress has been made and there are advantages to these forms of evidence, there are also disadvantages. It is the purpose of this write up to explore the advantages and disadvantages that have been brought about by the introduction of digital and DNA evidence in Zimbabwe.

Digital evidence is defined as information and data of value to an investigation that is stored on, received or transmitted by an electronic device. It is important to note that digital evidence is intangible. Electronic device include laptops, desktops, telephones and cellphones to mention a few. Due to technological advancements the scope of what encompasses electronic devices has widened which means there are many sources of digital evidence. Currently, in Zimbabwe, digital is being adduced under documentary evidence because the machines that produce them are the same. However the nature of documentary and digital evidence is different which makes them distinct. It is the left to court to decide what evidence is admissible. The Civil Evidence Act[1] and the Criminal Procedure and Evidence Act[2] do not provide for the admission of digital evidence however there are provisions for documentary evidence. One can argue that these provisions do not apply as digital evidence is intangible as opposed to documentary evidence. Strides have been made however

---

[1] Civil Evidence Act [Chapter 8:01]
[2] Criminal Procedure and Evidence Act [Chapter 9:01]

and there is legislation in progress like the Cyber Crimes Bill, Electronic Transactions and Electronic Transactions Bill and the Data Protection Bill which sanction for the adjudication of digital evidence.

DNA (deoxyribonucleic acid) is defined as a forensic technique used to identify individuals by the characteristics of their genetic makeup. Thus DNA evidence refers to evidence which relates to samples of the human body like saliva, blood and hair which can be adduced in a court of law. The Criminal Procedure and Evidence Act under section 41 allows for the admission of such evidence in court for criminal matters[3]. The Civil Evidence Act under section 22 allows for expert evidence and under 23 medical opinions which the courts use as grounds for admitting DNA evidence[4]. However, there is need for provisions which establish a clear position as far as DNA evidence is concerned in civil matters like the provisions in criminal matters. There is progress under the proposed DNA and Forensic Evidence Bill which will provide for the circumstances under which DNA evidence can be accepted in court thus providing guidance. DNA evidence in civil matters is being accepted as a result of the provision which allows for expert evidence and opinions. It requires the opinions of forensic experts.

To begin with, digital evidence has an advantage in that it has widened the laws of Zimbabwe in respect of criminal offences thus delivering justice. There are new challenges to legal proceedings where there are crimes that are being committed which can be prosecuted using digital evidence. Crimes like identity theft, distributing and making use of child pornography, identity theft, cyber bullying and credit card theft have become dominant in modern day. This in turn ensures the delivery of justice. Technological advancements has given criminals new ways to commit crimes and give birth to new crimes which require prosecution. Digital evidence has widened the law as is shown by the Computer Crime and Cybercrime Bill which is going to cater for most computer related crimes which can be prosecuted using digital evidence[5]. For example under section 14 of the bill there is the provision which relates to child pornography and it is made clear the circumstances where one is liable for that offence. Section 28 of the draft makes it clear that the fact that

---

[3] Ibid 2
[4] Ibid 1
[5] Computer Crime and Cybercrime Bill [draft]

evidence has been electronically generated is not grounds for inadmissibility. Other offences introduced are identity crimes and those relating to racist and xenophobic material. This a clear demonstration of how the adoption of digital evidence has widened the laws of Zimbabwe in respect of criminal offences.

On the other hand, digital evidence has the disadvantage of being prone to easy alterations and manipulations. Being an intangible form of evidence found on electronic devices, digital evidence can be easily altered and it does not register who has made the alterations which provides ground for challenging it[6]. This is because the originality and legitimacy of such evidence is thus highly questionable. One of the rules of evidence is that it must be logical and relevant to the matter in question which means where the legitimacy and originality of evidence is being questioned it is risky to admit it in a court of law. In the case of *S v Bennet* the same question with regards to digital evidence was raised[7]. There were emails that were alleged by the prosecution to have linked the accused person to the criminal enterprise that was in question. The defence challenged the legitimacy of these emails in that they had been fabricated and the expert was not well versed in those matters thus his opinion was not of much value. The court accepted these arguments and that those emails could have been created by anyone and where not enough evidence to convict the accused and no nexus between the accused and the charges, thus he was acquitted. This shows the danger in the adoption of digital evidence as it can be easily fabricated or manipulated thus implicating innocent persons.

The adoption of DNA evidence in Zimbabwe has brought the opportunity of convicting offenders in serious crimes like those of a sexual nature. Since DNA evidence is concerned with pointing out an individual by analyzing their genetic makeup, it is easier to identify criminals under this system. It is based on identifying the person on a scale of probabilities thus it is used to prove guilt with the inclusion of other forms of evidence. In the case of *S v R Willis* it was remarked that substantial benefits can be drawn from harnessing the advances in modern science to the law[8]. When it comes to rape case, DNA testing can be especially helpful. This shows that the court is also of the opinion that DNA evidence can be used as a

---

[6] P J Schikkard & S E Van de Merwe *Principles of Evidence*(2002) Juta
[7] HH-79-2010
[8] 2000 (1) SACR 33

medium to identify criminals effectively. G Feltoe is also of the same view that DNA evidence can be used to convict criminals. It also has the advantage of exonerating the wrongfully convicted[9]. There are people who are wrongfully convicted as criminals and DNA evidence can be used to distance such people from criminal activities. In Zimbabwe such lessons can be drawn from the innocence project in the United States of America which is a project which seeks to exonerate wrongly convicted persons[10]. It makes use of DNA evidence and extensive research to clarify if the state prosecuted the correct persons. To thus far, it can be seen that DNA evidence can be used to convict criminals and exonerate the wrongly convicted.

In a different light, DNA evidence has the challenge of being inaccurate at times. This is because this technique is based on a balance of probabilities or the chances of the existence of such a scenario. This means that an individual can be identified as the most likely in such a scenario but out there, there will be other individuals who are a most desirable match. To that there are grounds under which DNA can be challenged. It can also be added that DNA is not conclusive as a source of evidence. It does not provide an end to the matter, as there are other forms of evidence which must be put into consideration. According to Zeffert, the extraction of DNA evidence must be done with care and there is need to exercise sufficient clarity when recording results[11]. This shows that DNA evidence is highly prone to inaccuracy. DNA evidence is extracted from the human body thus prone to contamination by germs or bacteria which influence the outcome of the result.

Furthermore, the introduction digital evidence has an advantage as there has been a shift in ways in which people talk and communicate as well as share information. These platforms are where crimes are being committed and adducing them as evidence can help prosecute criminals. This is because these platforms are mostly related to the internet and electronic devices. There are emails, social media and telephones. On the platforms, criminal activities can actually happen. In the case of *Chirwa v Paradza* the prosecution sought to lead evidence in the form of a recorded telephone conversation[12]. The accused sought to challenge this in that it violated his rights to privacy. The court rejected this argument as it was not the law that evidence

---

[9] G Feltoe "Strengthening our Law on Child and Sexual Abuse" (2017)Part 1 *Zimbabwe Electronic Law Journal*
[10] https://www.innocenceproject.org (accessed 30 August 2017)
[11] D T Zeffert et al *The South African Law of Evidence* (2003) 4th ed
[12] SC 25/05

obtained as a result of unlawful interception of a telephone conversation must be excluded from court proceedings. The telephone call was the used as evidence in convicting the accused of corruption and perverting the course of justice which led to dismissal from office. To thus far, it can be seen that digital evidence in modern day can be used to prosecute criminals and convict them, since there are new ways through which people communicate and share information.

DNA evidence has brought about benefits in civil matters at it can be used to establish paternity. The courts have in modern times adjudicated upon claims of child support in which fathers deny paternity of the children thus escape their responsibility. However with the adoption of DNA evidence, it is now much easier to establish paternity thus making sure that a person takes responsibility of their actions. In an age where promiscuity and adultery are the order of the day in marital relations, DNA evidence comes in to assist the aggrieved weaker party. In the case of *Shumba v Shumba* the court enforced the judgement of the court a quo where paternity had been established using DNA evidence[13]. The appellant sought to challenge the judgement on this basis that there were supernatural forces that had tempered with the results thus there were not credible. He had also contended that the children were not his and that the one who had Down syndrome was a goblin. The court disregarded these arguments and enforced the DNA results. To that end, the introduction of DNA evidence has made the establishment of paternity in child support issues easy.

On the other hand, both DNA and digital evidence are answerable to the question of relevance and logic. This places it in the hand of the court to determine whether certain forms are admissible in certain circumstances. This in itself is a disadvantage as over reliance can be placed upon digital and DNA evidence even when it is unnecessary to do so. There is also ignorance of other forms of evidence in which case the court must analyse all the available evidence in order to reach a conclusion not placing over reliance on only one source. Although under the best evidence rule the best evidence must be admitted, this rule can be abused where there over reliance on one form of evidence which is in violation to the principles of natural justice. The court has a duty to see that justice is done and prevails and where there is overdependence on digital and DNA evidence, the courts have failed. To thus far,

---

[13] HB 25/05

the adoption of DNA and digital evidence in Zimbabwe has led to courts being dependent and placing little to no importance on other forms of evidence.

In Zimbabwe, a challenge to the admissibility of digital and DNA evidence is the lack of qualified personnel that is people who can interpret, test and clarify these forms of evidence. This presents a challenge in the legitimacy of these forms of evidence. Zimbabwe being a country that is still amidst technological advancements it is still yet to have trained people who can assist in such matters. In the case of S v Bennet the witness who was called upon to offer expert opinion was discredited by the court as under cross examinations he demonstrated of lack the knowledge which was needed by the court to accept the evidence as relevant[14]. The state witness was supposed to offer his opinion on the legitimacy of certain emails that were before the court. Even his academic qualifications were held to be insufficient for him to have knowledge of the technological issue that was at hand. This thus demonstrates the challenge of lack of qualified personnel which has been made apparent by the adoption of digital and DNA evidence in Zimbabwe. This works hand in glove with what has been termed as the CSI (criminal scene investigation) effect in modern circles[15]. As a result of movies and television shows the general public now has a misconception that all the people have a knowledge of how DNA and digital evidence works and this tends to be the incorrect thing as what is portrayed on television is far from reality. People now expect a perfect trail of evidence like on television. This means the public is unaware of how these issues work under actual court proceedings and there is need to raise awareness so that the people have an idea. As a result of the CSI effect people can also profess to have knowledge that they do not actually possess. As far as the introduction and adoption of DNA evidence is concerned this is a disadvantage.

In conclusion, it is clear that Zimbabwe is making great strides in introducing DNA and digital evidence as well as adopting it. There are factors however which affect this progress thus there has been benefits as well as non-benefits in the process. This is as result of the status of Zimbabwe as far as technological advancements are concerned, social issues and legal issues. Over and above, it can be seen that the process has brought about mixed results as the non-benefits equal the benefits.

---

[14] Ibid 6
[15] https://www.cbsnews.com/news/the-csi-effect/ (accessed 30 August 2017)

There is need to refine the procedures and circumstances under which DNA and digital evidence are admissible so as to fully reap the benefits of the introduction and adoption of these forms of evidence in Zimbabwe.

BIBLIOGRAPHY

BILLS

Computer Crimes and Cybercrimes Bill [draft]

BOOKS

Schikkard P J & Van de Merwe S E (2002) *Principle of Evidence,* Juta

Zeffert D T et al (2003) The South African Law of Evidence, 4th Ed, Butterworth's

FOREIGN CASE LAW

S v R Willis 2000 (1) SACR 33

JOURNAL ARTICLES

Feltoe G "Strengthening our Law on Child Sexual Abuse" (2017) Part 1 *Zimbabwe Electric Law Journal*

LEGISLATION

Civil Evidence Act [Chapter 8:01]

Criminal Procedure and Evidence Act [Chapter 9:01]

WEBSITES

https://www.cbsnews.com/news/the-csi-effect/ (accessed 30 August 2017)

https://www.innocenceproject.org (accessed 30 August 2017)

ZIMBABWEAN CASE LAW

Paradza v Chirwa SC 25/05

S V Bennet HH 79/10

Shumba v Shumba HB 25/05

YOUR KNOWLEDGE HAS VALUE